PRESENTED TO:

_____

BY:

_____

DATE:

_____

101 SIMPLE SECRETS

TO KEEP YOUR

HOPE ALIVE

HONOR HB BOOKS

Inspiration and Motivation for the Season of Life

An Imprint of Cook Communications Ministries • Colorado Springs, CO

08 07 06 05 04   10 9 8 7 6 5 4 3 2 1

101 Simple Secrets to Keep Your Hope Alive
ISBN 1-56292-134-7

Copyright © 2003 Bordon Books
An imprint of Cook Communications Ministry
4050 Lee Vance View
Colorado Springs, Colorado 80918

Developed by Bordon Books

Manuscript compiled by Betsy Williams, Tulsa, Oklahoma, in conjunction with Bordon Books.

INTRODUCTION

In the midst of school shootings, terrorist attacks, and a shaky economy, it would be easy to become hopeless. But there's good news! None of the troubling circumstances that fill our world surprise God. What better way to keep your hope alive than a book filled with 101 ways to remind you that God is there for you and He is on your side. *101 Simple Secrets to Keep Your Hope Alive,* offers a touch of divine hope and allows you to see through your challenging days. This book of hope is a fresh collection of insights to help readers see beyond their human struggles to God's goodness. A corresponding scripture or encouraging quote accompanies each simple secret. You will be amazed at how a few simple changes will encourage your outlook. God loves you, and He knows just what you're going through. So get your hopes up! God will never let you down.

1

LAUGH MORE—
ESPECIALLY AT YOURSELF.

cheerful heart is a good medicine.

PROVERBS 17:22 NRSV

Laughter promotes good health, both in body and spirit. It not only brightens your mood, but also eases tension. A good dose of laughter has been shown to improve blood circulation, stimulate digestion, lower blood pressure, and prompt the brain to release pain-reducing endorphins.

Laughter is also a sign that you place your hope in God instead of the changing circumstances around you. It is the best response you can make to your own human frailties as you strive to live a hope-filled life.

LAUGHTER IS THE CHEAPEST, SAFEST, AND MOST RELIABLE MEDICATION THERE IS.

2

PRACTICE SPEAKING POSITIVELY.

A word can be a balm or a bomb.
A positive word makes you feel good.
A negative word leaves you
feeling depressed and defeated.

It's been said that the default mode of most people's thinking is negative. If you're not aware of it, those negative thoughts can easily become negative talk. Take a personal inventory. Do you tend to be an optimist or a pessimist by nature? Do you tend to think encouraging or discouraging thoughts most of the time?

If you lean toward the pessimistic side, try more positive speech. Pay attention to your thought patterns and work to reverse negative thinking. Read books or utilize other materials that enhance positive thought patterns. You can be an up person in a down world.

BE A POSITIVE LIGHT IN A DARK
AND NEGATIVE WORLD.

3

FEED YOUR SOUL WITH A DOSE OF CREATION'S BEAUTY.

Beauty is a gift of God.

A woman on her way to work one chilly, overcast winter morning was startled to see a patch of pansies in bloom. Their glorious purple and yellow hues were a stark contrast to the cloudy skies. Her mood instantly brightened. Those delicate flowers reminded her that there is always hope, even on the gloomiest of days and in the darkest of times.

When you take your eyes off your problems—even for a moment—you often find that God has placed something glorious in your path to cheer you on your way. Look around you. What can you see in your path that brightens your day today?

TO GET YOUR HOPES UP, OPEN YOUR EYES TO SEE WHAT GOD SEES.

4

TREAT YOUR BODY RIGHT.

Look to your health; and if you have it,
praise God, and value it next
to a good conscience; for health is
the second blessing that we mortals
are capable of; a blessing that
money cannot buy.

Busy schedules sometimes mean that attention to exercise and good nutrition fall through the cracks. Anyone can have a lapse, but the wise understand that neglecting the proper care of our bodies can put our sense of well-being at risk.

Both exercise and nutrition are inextricably related to an internal sense of balance and emotional calm. Both are vital to energy levels, strength, and basic good health; and both can have a direct effect on how hopeful or hopeless we feel. Keeping yourself built up and running at peak performance will help you to remain hopeful when the firestorms of life come your way.

AS THE BODY GAINS STRENGTH, SO DOES THE INNER SELF.

5

GIVE YOURSELF PERMISSION
TO SAY NO.

This will we do, if God permit.

HEBREWS 6:3 KJV

We live in a society that is constantly challenging us to stretch beyond our limits and reach for the stars. Pleas for help as well as demands on our time and energies lie around every corner. It's easy to feel overwhelmed. Eventually, we each have to accept the fact that no one can do it all. Freedom comes when we learn to say no.

Saying no frees you to say yes to those things that bring the greatest satisfaction and sense of well-being. It also allows you to de-clutter your life and restore balance. It is the first step to leading a simpler, more productive life.

HEALTHY BOUNDARIES ALLOW US TO BE TRUE TO WHO WE ARE AND WHAT WE ARE MEANT TO DO.

6

INVEST YOUR RESOURCES IN
THINGS OF LASTING VALUE.

"Where your treasure is,
there your heart
will be also."

MATTHEW 6:21

It's a wise person who stops along the way to ask, "What resources do I have, and how am I investing them?" Resources consist of more than finances. They also include time, love, energy, and everything else that God has given you.

Take time on a regular basis for a reality check. Are you responding to those things that seem urgent and neglecting those things that are most important? Wise investments now will produce results you can live with, giving you hope for the future.

INVESTING IN THINGS OF ETERNAL VALUE WILL PRODUCE EVERLASTING RESULTS.

7

GIVE YOURSELF A BREAK.

To err is human,
to forgive,
divine.

When faced with a challenge, it is always wise to ask for God's help, prepare to the best of your ability, give your most worthy effort—and then cut yourself some slack! No one gets everything right every time; perfection belongs to God alone.

As difficult as it may be to accept, everyone fails sometimes, even when they try hard to do well. The good news is that most people learn more from their failures than from their successes, and failure can create greater empathy and sensitivity toward others.

If you ask for forgiveness, God forgives and forgets your error. So give yourself a break. Forgive yourself today!

FORGIVING YOURSELF WILL
SET YOUR HEART FREE.

8

PLANT SOMETHING AND
WATCH IT GROW.

*Like the number of apples contained
in an apple seed,
each opportunity we seize holds
an untold number of possibilities.*

Remember the simple assignment from elementary school—plant seeds in a cup of dirt, and watch them grow? Did it seem unbelievable that a tiny seed could become a beautiful flower or tasty vegetable? What a delight to water the soil, put the small pot in the sun, and watch the first green shoots emerge. You witnessed the miracle of *life*.

That joyful experience is easy to recapture. Find a small pot, fill it with soil, and plant your seeds. Then watch as new life breaks forth. Let it encourage you.

WHERE THERE IS LIFE, THERE IS HOPE.

9

BEGIN AND END EACH DAY WITH GENUINE THANKSGIVING TO GOD.

Enter into his gates with thanksgiving,
and *into his courts with praise:*
be thankful unto him,
and *bless his name.*

PSALM 100:4 KJV

Nothing fans the flame of hope more than acknowledging the good things in your life and thanking God for them. Even when circumstances are grim, you can always find something to be thankful for. Why is this important? Human nature causes you to focus on the negative, and the negative overwhelms your sense of inner contentment.

Rehearsing the positive aspects of your life will help you restore a delicate emotional balance and stabilize your inner compass. There is no better way to gain perspective and keep your hopes up.

COUNT YOUR MANY BLESSINGS. NAME THEM ONE BY ONE!

10

SEEK OUT A MENTOR.

The older women . . . can train the younger women.

TITUS 2:3-4

A mentoring relationship is one in which someone who has been through similar life experiences can be an empathetic shoulder to lean on and an encouraging coach to help you navigate life's challenges.

Generally speaking, experience comes with age, and wisdom comes from experience. If you know of someone who has been through some of the life passages you are facing, ask the person to share with you over lunch or coffee. Don't become discouraged if your first choice does not have the time or interest in a mentoring relationship. Pray for the right match to come along.

NO ONE CAN ENCOURAGE YOU LIKE SOMEONE WHO'S BEEN THERE.

11

CONSISTENTLY CULTIVATE
TIMES OF SOLITUDE.

Alone with God! It is there that what is
hid with God is made known—
God's ideals, God's hopes,
God's doings.

As a vessel takes shape on a potter's wheel, the potter applies pressure to both the inside and the outside of the pot as it spins. Without the inside pressure, the pot would collapse inward. Without the outside pressure, the pot would not retain any shape.

People also need strength from the inside to withstand the everyday pressures exerted from the outside. When we spend regular time in quiet solitude, listening to the heartbeat of God, we receive strength to withstand the pressures of life. Then we are better able to respond to crises with confidence.

SOLITUDE STRENGTHENS
AND RENEWS THE SOUL AS
FOOD AND SLEEP STRENGTHEN
AND RENEW THE BODY.

12

PUT THINGS BACK
WHERE YOU GOT THEM.

If you can organize your kitchen,
you can organize your life.

Who can fully calculate the time wasted looking for misplaced keys, tickets, eyeglasses, records needed for tax preparation, or an appliance warranty? Not to mention trying to find that elusive other sock, shoe, or earring. Returning something to its rightful place turns out to be an amazing investment when you think of it that way.

Save yourself from the stress and frustration of searching for what you need. Designate a place for each and every item, and send it home each time you use it. You will be amazed at how this one little change can bring peace to your life. You can then use that energy for more important tasks.

NO LONGER AGONIZE.
ORGANIZE!

13

SMILE AT STRANGERS.

Keep a smile on your face.

ROMANS 12:8 THE MESSAGE

Few actions require so little and give back so much as a smile! Your smile to a stranger may be the only bright spot in that person's day, and there's a bonus in that smile for you as well. That's the great thing about smiles; they inspire happiness in both the receiver and the sender.

Add the "smile factor" to your daily routine for one week. Smile when you pass people; smile at people in the elevator; smile at the motorist in the next car. Smile—smile—smile! You are sure to find your world less intimidating, your interactions with others more satisfying, and your overall outlook greatly improved.

A SMILE BRIGHTENS
EVERYONE'S DAY.

14

IDENTIFY YOUR MOST PRODUCTIVE TIME OF DAY AND MAXIMIZE IT.

Make it thy business to know thyself.

Metabolisms vary, energy levels ebb and flow, and body rhythms fluctuate. A major key to maintaining a balanced sense of well-being is to recognize and work with your own natural, internal body rhythms. It will enable you to maximize efficiency and productivity and help you take charge of your life.

Schedule the most challenging tasks when energy is at a peak level. Don't let anything interfere with these important hours—making the most of them can be a key to success.

When energy and creativity begin to wane, take a break or switch to more routine chores. And when you feel the need, take a nap.

FIND OUT WHAT MAKES
YOU TICK AND LIVE
YOUR LIFE ACCORDINGLY.

15

GIVE WHAT YOU DON'T NEED
TO SOMEONE WHO NEEDS IT.

*The measure of life is not its duration
but its donation.
How much will you be missed?*

Go to your pantry and put your hand on a few cans of food that have been there for a while. Then go to any closet, drawer, or storage space in your home, and pull out things you don't use. You're sure to find some items that you didn't even remember you owned.

Now consider this. Within a small radius of your home, no matter *where* you live, you will be able to find people who have little or nothing at all. Meeting someone else's need, even in a small way, will inspire hope in them, and it will be an incredibly gratifying experience for you as well.

GIVE HOPE TO OTHERS—
IT WILL DO WONDERS
FOR YOU TOO.

16

THANK SOMEONE!

ive thanks to the LORD,

for he is good.

PSALM 118:1

No one is an island. From the day you were born until the day you die, you are dependent upon the help of others in countless ways. Who taught you to tie your shoes and button your shirt? Who stuck with you until you mastered long division or learned to read? Who encouraged you and helped you land your first job? Who taught you to love selflessly or encouraged you to use your talents to make a difference in the world?

As you grow older, your need for others becomes more acute. Your gratitude should grow in like measure. Today is a good day to send a note of thanks to someone who inspired you.

DEVELOP AN ATTITUDE OF GRATITUDE.

17

BE ALERT FOR THE "SMALL MIRACLES" THAT HAPPEN EVERY DAY.

Lord! How Thy wonders are displayed
Where'er I turn mine eye.

Miracles happen all around us every day. So often, that we routinely overlook them in the moment. It may be hours later that you realize God's miraculous protection surrounded you. Perhaps upon quiet reflection you recognize that being on time for an appointment despite numerous detours or finding a person in a crowd had a truly miraculous element to it.

Sometimes the miracles around you are as simple as a bud bursting into bloom or the hatching of birds' eggs outside your kitchen window. Taking time to *see* and appreciate the miraculous is guaranteed to bring a smile to your soul and hope to your heart.

MIRACLES ARE ALL AROUND. CAN YOU SEE THEM?

18

PREPARE FOR STRESS.

"*God will help you deal with whatever hard things come up when the time comes.*"

MATTHEW 6:34 THE MESSAGE

Stress happens. Daily. To everyone—including you. Along with good old, everyday traffic jams and annoying telemarketers, your life will sometimes hit more than just a bump in the road. You may be dealing with unemployment, divorce, illness, a new baby, or a death in the family. And your body knows it.

The best way to deal with stress and keep from feeling overwhelmed is to beat stress before it beats you. Develop healthy habits in diet, sleep, and exercise. Invest the time it takes to build healthy relationships. Recognize God's sovereignty over your life. When an unexpected crisis catches you off guard, give yourself a break. Cut out the nonessentials, and take the time you need to get your feet back on solid ground.

DISTRESS IS MOST OFTEN STRESS THAT HASN'T BEEN ADDRESSED.

19

REJOICE WITH THOSE WHO REJOICE.

I am glad and rejoice with all of you.
So you too should be glad
and rejoice with me.

PHILIPPIANS 2:17-18

Many people find it easier to weep with those who weep than to rejoice with those who rejoice, because jealousy has a way of rearing its ugly head. Yet a sure way to keep your hopes high is to celebrate the good things that come into the lives of others—allow their delight to become your delight.

If you truly are in relationship with other people, what they experience *is,* quite literally, a part of your experience. To count the good that happens to them as partly your own—without giving in to selfish impulses—will allow you to grow very rich, indeed, in joy, hope, and happiness.

TO MULTIPLY YOUR OWN JOY, ENJOY THE HAPPINESS OF OTHERS.

20

GIVE YOURSELF A BOUQUET
OF FRESH FLOWERS.

Flowers are the sweetest things
God ever made and
forgot to put a soul into.

Nothing brightens a room or one's mood quite like a bouquet of fresh flowers! Flowers provide a splash of vibrant color to brighten the day and remind you of the beauty God placed in the world. Flowers also speak of the fragility and delicacy of life and coax you to abandon your striving after the vain and temporal. They echo the splendors of Eden and are a promise of the glory of Heaven. Even more, flowers demonstrate God's wisdom and power. After all, who can make a flower but God?

As the English statesman William Wilberforce once said, "Lovely flowers are the smiles of God's goodness."

GIVE YOURSELF A REMINDER
OF THE GOODNESS AND
BEAUTY GOD HAS CREATED.

21

GO FLY A KITE!

ou will soon break the bow if you keep it always stretched.

Charles Schulz, creator of the *Peanuts* comic series, once noted that the reason he drew images of childhood is because most people can relate to moments when they were carefree and the biggest problem in life was keeping the kite out of the neighbor's tree.

On the next windy day, build or buy a kite, go to the nearest open field, let out the string, and let all your cares and worries go *up, up, up,* and *away.* Forget your adult responsibilities for a few minutes, and recapture the essence of unfettered happiness.

TO FLY A KITE, YOU HAVE TO LOOK UP!

22

CHOOSE TO SEE THE
BEST IN OTHERS.

*L ove . . . always looks
for the best.*

1 CORINTHIANS 13:4-7 THE MESSAGE

Life is about choices, and one of the more important ones is how you view other people. You can choose to focus on an individual's good points or keep your eyes on those things that annoy you. You can choose to acknowledge and praise an individual's gifts, talents, and contributions, or choose to stay blind to the positive characteristics and see only their faults.

How you choose to see others, to a very great extent, reflects your opinion of your own self-worth. It also affects how you feel about the world in general. To choose to see the good in yourself and in others is to acknowledge that God is the giver of all good gifts. It is something you can do to make your world a brighter place.

LOOK FOR THE BEST IN SOMEONE, AND THEN TELL THEM WHAT YOU SEE.

23

EXERCISE, EXERCISE, EXERCISE.

Those who think they have not time for bodily exercise will sooner or later have to find time for illness.

The human body is like the battery-toting bunny in television commercials—it will keep going and going and going if it is connected to the right energy source. Disregard the body's basic needs, however, and it will burn out and cease to function. One of the basic needs your body craves is regular exercise—heart-stimulating, blood-pumping, endorphin-raising activity.

While exercise may seem inconvenient, boring, or tedious at times, its benefits are abundant; and keeping your body at its peak is sure to enhance your general sense of well-being. What are you waiting for—get up and get going! One and two and one and two and. . . .

EXERCISE YOUR RIGHT
TO A BETTER LIFE.

24

GUARD YOUR REST.

---

*The end and the reward
of toil is rest.*

The society we live in seems determined to pack as much as possible into every day—work, recreation, family time, good deeds—everything, it seems, but rest and relaxation. Our hectic lifestyles seem shortsighted in light of the fact that physicians say rest enhances the enjoyment and effectiveness of all our other efforts.

Rest, both physical and mental, will render you more alert, more productive, more efficient, and less irritable—in a word, happier! Use it as a baseline for all your other activities. Your body will thank you for it.

A NAP IS A TERRIBLE
THING TO WASTE!

25

START THE DAY BY
READING THE BIBLE.

Your word is a lamp to my feet and a light for my path.

PSALM 119:105

"Eat a good breakfast," that's what our moms used to say. Good nutrition in the morning imparts energy and strength for the entire day. That's the case with our spiritual energy and strength as well. Many believe that the Bible is the best source of spiritual nutrition, and at the very least, its pages are filled with sublime prose, extraordinary poetry, and practical wisdom.

As you begin, think about how each Scripture might apply specifically to you and the situations you face. Let them build hope in you. The truths of the Bible are ageless and offer powerful guidance as you go through your days, weeks, and years. They will help you keep your hope alive.

GO FROM HOPELESS
TO HOPEFUL—
READ THE BIBLE.

26

START SOMETHING AND FINISH IT.

Success lies in the finishing,
not the dreaming
or the starting.

"There!" and "Whew!" are two of the most satisfying exclamations in the English language, especially when they punctuate the completion of a difficult task. Bringing a project or chore to completion evokes feelings of satisfaction, relief, and inner pride. Procrastination, on the other hand, is like a gray cloud that hangs over everything you do and dampens your spirits.

Someplace in your home or office is a task that has just been sitting there waiting for you to come along and tackle it. Don't put it off; dive in and get it done! You'll be glad you did. And the good feeling you get when you get something done will light a glimmer of hope that you'll get other things finished as well.

FEW THINGS ARE MORE SATISFYING THAN A JOB WELL DONE.

27

RECOGNIZE THAT HAPPINESS IS A CHOICE.

Most folks are about as happy as they make up their minds to be.

Scarlett O'Hara, the foremost character in the classic *Gone with the Wind,* believed that only one thing would make her happy—becoming Mrs. Ashley Wilkes. When Ashley married another woman, rather than make the most of things, Scarlett threw her happiness away with both hands.

Happiness is an emotion, but it is greatly influenced by the choices you make. You can choose to be optimistic rather than pessimistic, hopeful rather than doubtful. Sure, life will throw you some curve balls, but no one can steal your happiness.

Putting your hope in God will also help you stay on the positive side of things. There are many scriptures in the Bible that attest to His faithfulness to help in times of need, so turn your back on misery today.

THERE'S ALWAYS SOMETHING TO BE HAPPY ABOUT. EMBRACE THAT SOMETHING TODAY.

28

SCHEDULE A "MENTAL HEALTH DAY" EACH QUARTER.

All work and no play makes Jack a dull boy and doesn't leave Jill with much of a shine either.

Try spending an entire day doing what is enjoyable, luxuri-
ous, special, and rewarding to your inner soul. It may be spending a day with dear friends or walking in a beautiful setting,
soaking in bubbles or taking an afternoon nap, curling up with a
good book or watching an old movie. Whatever it is, take time to
truly relax and enjoy a break from the busyness of life. Focus on
things eternal, meaningful, and joyful.

These periodic personal retreats are guaranteed to make you
feel refreshed and more balanced. They will give you a renewed
outlook and a fresh willingness to tackle the tasks at hand.

TIME OFF TO GET IN TOUCH
WITH YOURSELF AND GOD
IS TIME WELL SPENT.

29

CONTACT AN OLD FRIEND
AND GET REACQUAINTED.

---

*The best mirror is an
old friend.*

Friends from times past, especially from childhood, offer a unique perspective on your life. They are associated with memories marked by greater innocence and purity. Lifelong friends are likely to be familiar with our family members, culture, church, school, or neighborhood. Getting back in touch can complete a circle, of sorts—providing a sense of wholeness, meaning, perspective, and personal warmth.

Friendships give us comfort and encouragement to face the future. Old friendships renewed also give the comfort and solace of times past.

RECLAIM THE JOY OF THE PAST— CALL AN OLD FRIEND!

30

PURSUE A LONG-NEGLECTED DREAM.

A longing fulfilled is sweet to the soul.

PROVERBS 13:19

Anna longed to be an artist. Though she lacked paint, she used berry juice to satisfy her passion. Unfortunately, after her marriage, she was forced to set her hobby aside. Life on the family farm, especially with a husband and children, kept her busy around the clock. She found a few minutes for embroidery in the evenings, but arthritis eventually made that pastime painful. Long past retirement age, she decided to return to her childhood joy. She picked up a paintbrush once again, and at age seventy-eight began to sell her work.

Anna—whom we know as Grandma Moses—proved that it's never too late to find success and happiness doing something you love.

TODAY IS THE DAY TO GO AFTER YOUR DREAM.

31

MAKE A NEW FRIEND.

Friendship adds a brighter radiance to prosperity and lightens the burden of adversity.

One of life's great blessings is to relax in the comfortable presence of old friends, where you are loved and accepted simply for who you are. You may forget, however, that it was not always so. These dear and constant ones were once "new friends." God sent them across your path so that you might expand your horizons and grow in new ways.

If you are wise, you will extend yourself to others and seek to forge new friendships. The older you are, the more difficult this might seem. But the rewards are great, and you are sure to find yourself refreshed and challenged.

ENLARGE YOUR CIRCLE OF JOY.
MAKE A NEW FRIEND.

32

SCHEDULE A "TEA TIME"
EVERY DAY.

Rest is not quitting the busy career;
rest is the fitting of
self to one's sphere.

A corporation once instituted a "teacart" policy—several persons pushed teacarts along the company hallways, pouring hot tea and offering small, sweet treats free-of-charge to employees around three o'clock in the afternoon. The result was a dramatic increase in both productivity and quality of work during the remainder of the workday. Employees also registered a marked increase in their satisfaction with the firm and with their jobs.

Teatime provided four positive things for the employees: a restful break, a brief time to socialize with coworkers, a perceived "reward," and an energy boost. We all need these four things at least once a day! Suggest it to your boss, or prepare teatime for yourself.

TIME OUT FOR TEA
CAN REFUEL YOU FOR
THE REST OF THE DAY.

33

BUY SOMETHING WHIMSICAL
AT A GARAGE SALE.

"Love your neighbor as yourself."

MARK 12:31

The words of Jesus Christ recorded in the Bible admonish us to love others *as we love ourselves.* This perhaps runs contrary to the way many you may have been taught, but ultimately it makes sense. You will be kinder to others when you have first been kind to yourself.

So don't be afraid to indulge in the occasional childlike pleasure, as long as it presents no danger for you or others. And these adventures in self-aggrandizement need not break the bank. A few cents for a garage sale treasure can leave you with a happy heart.

GIVE YOURSELF A GIFT TODAY
FOR NO REASON AT ALL!

34

PAY AS YOU GO.

Let no debt remain outstanding,

except the continuing

debt to love one another.

ROMANS 13:8

Reader's Digest once reprinted an article from *Money* magazine entitled, "Win Your War Against Debt." In the middle of the article, there was a two-page advertisement for a popular antidepressant! The irony of the placement of this ad may not have been intentional, but it conveyed a truth—debt can be depressing. Almost nothing zaps your hope like a stack of unpaid bills marked "past due."

Some debt is unavoidable, but most indebtedness is self-inflicted. And if you get in too deep, paying off the debt can seem hopeless. A pay-as-you-go policy is the best way to get out of debt and stay out of debt. And the joy of a debt-free life cannot be calculated.

HAPPINESS CANNOT
BE PURCHASED!

35

AVOID GOSSIP.

There is nothing that can't be made worse by telling.

Good news travels fast and bad news travels faster. For some reason, people are more willing to pass along the negative things they hear than the positive. In so doing, they lose out on the positive return, for everything they say comes back to them eventually.

The road to true happiness is paved with compliments and praise. Such words bring hope and encouragement to both the speaker and the hearer. The positive things you say can also establish your reputation as a person of integrity, winning you the trust, admiration, and respect of others.

POSITIVE WORDS CREATE
A POSITIVE LIFE.

36

REINFORCE GOOD HABITS
AND DUMP BAD ONES.

---

*Cultivate only the habits
you are willing
should master you.*

Good health, good relationships—the good life, in general, is never an accident. It is the clear and simple result of good living. When you establish habits that keep your life on the right track, you can expect renewed hope to be a by-product.

Of course, it isn't possible to control every aspect of your life. There will be times of sorrow and pain, even calamity, that will come simply because we live in an imperfect world. Nonetheless, if you establish good habits, you will be able to maximize and protect what God has given you. And remember, it only takes twenty-one days to establish a good habit.

IN BUILDING GOOD HABITS, ONE BUILDS A GOOD LIFE.

37

CHOOSE A CAREER BASED ON PERSONAL SATISFACTION RATHER THAN EARNING POTENTIAL.

He is well paid that is well satisfied.

The ingredients necessary to produce genuine happiness vary from person to person, but one thing is true for all—material wealth or possessions never fully satisfy the inner longings of the human heart. Neither do they establish self-worth nor fulfill our inner need for love.

Each person is a wonderful combination of distinct talents and passions, fitted together with a deep desire to express their God-given uniqueness. Take time to search out your own special giftedness, and use it. It's a good way to keep hope alive.

DOING WHAT YOU WERE CREATED TO DO RESULTS IN SATISFACTION THAT MONEY CAN'T BUY.

38

SEE THE WORLD—EVEN IF IT'S ONLY YOUR NEIGHBORHOOD.

Voyage, travel, and change of place impart vigor.

Think for a moment about those places you would most like to see, and map a plan for going there. Another state? Another nation? Why live like a hamster running in a wheel, running in the same rut every day to the same places at the same times? Take a time out! Establish a timetable for embarking on your personal adventure. The truth is that hope can be borne out of your anticipation. So build your hopes up, and dream big!

And in the meantime, take time out to discover the treasures in your own backyard and neighborhood. There's an amazing world just a few miles from you that is waiting to be discovered and enjoyed.

DISCOVER THE WORLD OF ADVENTURE THAT IS RIGHT AROUND YOU.

39

DO A GOOD DEED FOR
SOMEONE IN NEED.

A good man produces good deeds from a good heart.

LUKE 6:45 TLB

Organizations like Habitat for Humanity have found that if fifty people join together, they can build or refurbish a house for a needy family. And if building a house is not quite your cup of tea, there are plenty of other organizations that will allow you to invest your time, energies, and talents in a good cause without having to bear the entire responsibility or expense.

Look for a project in your neighborhood or town. If you can't find one that seems right for you, start your own and invite others to take part. There is nothing quite as gratifying as the selfless act of helping others—nothing that will remind you so boldly of all God's goodness in your own life.

INSPIRING HOPE IN OTHERS WILL FAN THE FIRES OF HOPE IN YOUR OWN LIFE.

40

READ OR LISTEN TO
INSPIRING MATERIALS.

---

*W*hat would any of us do without books
and poems that help us along our way,
the books we return to again and again,
the poems we learn by heart
and repeat for comfort
in sleepless nights?

We all *need* inspiration—to persevere in the search for excellence, to continue in the struggle, and to endure through hard times. Perhaps someone will inspire you today. But if you're wise, you won't leave that to chance. Go out and find one of the numerous inspirational books, tapes, or videotapes available to help you stay the course and fulfill your potential. Such materials can help you get through a hard time or give you hope for a return of enthusiasm if you've suffered a setback.

Everyone needs an emotional boost occasionally, a pick-me-up, or a shove in the right direction. There's no fault in losing inspiration—only in allowing it to remain lost.

INSPIRING MATERIALS
ARE LIKE FERTILIZER
TO THE SEEDS OF HOPE.

41

TACKLE DIFFICULT CHORES FIRST.

*Far and away the best prize
that life offers is the
chance to work hard
at work worth doing.*

Whatever you find most difficult to do—take it on *first*. It's best to tackle tougher tasks early in the day when energy and motivation are both at peak levels. This little trick will help you complete jobs quicker with fewer complications. Plus, getting the tough task out of the way gives satisfaction and momentum to the rest of the day.

You may think you would be happiest with no chores at all. Perhaps you're right, but that would not be the case with most people. Work and the satisfaction it brings seem to be key ingredients needed to fuel the hope in our lives.

DON'T WORK HARDER;
WORK SMARTER!

42

REWARD YOURSELF FOR WORTHY GOALS OR DEEDS.

The labourer is worthy of his reward.

1 TIMOTHY 5:18 KJV

Rewards motivate most people to keep doing what they know to be good, right, and just. They help you to overcome the inertia of laziness and apathy. For that reason, you can use personal rewards as a way to increase your capacity for doing the right things.

As the old song declares, "Accentuate the positive . . . eliminate the negative!" The more you reward the positive, the more you turn your attention and efforts away from those negative things that pull you down and toward those uplifting things that bring hope and fulfillment.

REWARD YOURSELF WHEN YOU ACHIEVE YOUR GOAL. YOU DESERVE IT!

43

GIVE AND RECEIVE MORE HUGS.

The recommended daily requirement for hugs is: four per day for survival, eight per day for maintenance, and twelve per day for growth.

Hugs are powerful—they can take the hurt out of a child's scraped knee, heal a long-standing alienation, soothe a troubled soul, comfort the grieving heart, and put a smile on the face of almost any person who gives or receives one. Hugs are an expression of love without words. They speak for themselves, saying, "I care," "I accept you," "I value you," "I've missed you," "I like to be with you," "I'm here for you."

Hugs are necessary for emotional growth and well being. In fact, some researchers have concluded that children need as many hugs a day as they need glasses of milk. And marriage counselors often prescribe that spouses should hug at least twice a day. Whom do you plan to hug today?

HUMAN TOUCH CONNECTS US SPIRITUALLY AND PHYSICALLY TO OTHERS.

44

PLAY A GAME WITH A CHILD.

*We find delight in the beauty and
happiness of children
that makes the heart
too big for the body.*

Children play spontaneously and freely for the sheer fun of it. Many adults think that such play is childish, a waste of valuable time. The truth is that we could all use an occasional adventure into the innocence and unfettered delight of a child's world.

Find a little person and ask if they have any fun games that the two of you could play together. You might be surprised how much joy such an activity can produce—after all, there's nothing to prove and plenty to gain. Even if you lose, you're sure to come away smiling, and the level of your hope and expectancy will have gone up.

LIGHTEN UP.
HAVE FUN!

45

TAKE COOKIES TO A FRIEND OR NEIGHBOR.

The heart benevolent and kind the most resembles God.

Food has been an important means of expressing acceptance and hospitality in virtually every culture throughout recorded history. It is such a natural act that a young child is likely to offer a half-eaten cracker to a stranger.

There are undoubtedly many complex reasons why human beings feel this need to share; however, it is enough for us to know that such an exercise brings with it a strong sense of well-being. Somehow when you offer a kind gesture to someone else, it comes back to perch on your own windowsill!

NEED A PICK-ME-UP?
MAKE SOMEONE ELSE'S DAY.

46

SMILE THE MOMENT YOU WAKE UP IN THE MORNING.

The more you are thankful for what you have, the more you have to be thankful for.

Set a tone of happiness for the day by smiling as soon as you wake up each morning. First, smile at God, saying in your heart, *Thank You for watching over me all night.* Second, smile at the remembrance of at least one good thing that happened the day before. Third, smile at the thought of all the opportunities and blessings that await you during the day. Fourth, smile at the thought that God will be present throughout the day to help you with every crisis, challenge, or obstacle. Fifth, smile at the very fact that you are alive and *smiling.*

And since you will have so many smiles, be sure and give some away!

IT'S HARD TO BE DOWN IN THE DUMPS WHEN THERE'S A SMILE ON YOUR FACE.

47

LEARN SOMETHING NEW EVERY DAY.

Learning is discovering

a new world,

a new galaxy,

a new species.

It keeps you ageless.

Graduation ceremonies are called "commencement exercises," because they mark the beginning rather than the end of a learning process. Formal education simply equips people with the skills necessary to process information and expand their minds throughout their lifetime. Learning never ends!

The more we learn, the more we want to learn! The person who makes it a habit to learn something new every day awakens with a true zest for living—an expectancy and eagerness to discover even more about the world that God has created and those He has placed in it. Is there something you've always wanted to learn? Go ahead and learn it! You'll build hope into your life by pursuing a new interest.

DEVELOP A YEARNING
FOR LEARNING.

48

FOCUS ON THE BEST IN YOURSELF.

---

*Praise yourself daringly,
something always sticks.*

Most people tend to focus on those aspects of their personality and appearance that they would most like to change. Admit it. Don't you hear yourself saying something like, *If only my feet were smaller, my hair thicker, and my ears flatter.* That kind of thinking only leads to dissatisfaction and low self-esteem.

The one who keeps hope alive will find a way to focus on those things that others admire and like most about them—and celebrate those qualities! Focusing on your best characteristics can actually help you to see your life in a better light. After all, we are each God's unique creation.

BUILD THE GOOD THAT YOU ARE INTO THE BEST YOU CAN BE.

49

PRACTICE A LIFESTYLE
OF GENEROSITY.

A generous man will prosper;
he who refreshes others
will himself be refreshed.

PROVERBS 11:25

Truly optimistic people are routinely generous. Whether they have little or much, they have discovered the joy of sharing with others freely and abundantly. Such people are sometimes short on cash, but they are always rich in the things that money cannot buy.

Practice generosity in your own life. If you are already a generous person, press yourself to become even more generous. You will soon notice that your attitudes about money and possessions are changing, your relationships are flourishing, and your outlook on life is bright.

GIVING IS A RICH
WAY OF LIVING.

50

REGARD AGE AS A GIFT.

---

*Nothing is more beautiful
than cheerfulness
in an old face.*

There is a lot more to growing older than just adding wrinkles, submitting to aches and pains, and watching your children leave home. Age is a record of your days. And it bears *gifts*—namely wisdom and confidence.

So continue to celebrate those birthdays. Think back over the challenges you have conquered in the past year. Remember the victories, and cherish new accomplishments. Catalog the insights you've recently acquired, thank God for every day He has given you, and build your hope for many more.

LET IT BE SAID THAT YOU ARE AGED TO PERFECTION.

51

USE THINGS AND LOVE PEOPLE.

*Love seeks to make happy
rather than
to be happy.*

We live in a consumer culture—one that values possessions and experiences more than people. And yet, somehow we know that these things can never give to the human heart what it desires most—loving relationships and a sense of self-worth.

To keep hope alive, it is necessary to strike a balance between the pursuit of things and a solid investment in the lives of others. The best of all plans is to *use things* for the purpose of expressing love to others.

TRUE WEALTH CAN'T BE MEASURED IN DOLLARS AND CENTS.

52

OBSERVE A BUTTERFLY.

Those who hope in the LORD will renew their strength. They will soar on wings like eagles.

ISAIAH 40:31

Until the Wright brothers did what seemed impossible, people were unable to take to the skies. How far we have flown since then! And yet, no flying machine has ever matched the beauty of a butterfly, as it colors the air of a garden with its vibrantly designed wings.

The mystery and beauty of the butterfly lies beyond its ability to fly—it is in its miraculous transformation from a lowly caterpillar. Through its example you discover that the grounded and limited *can* soar to great heights, the bound and lifeless *can* be free and vibrant, and the dull and colorless *can* become beautiful and inspiring. Observe a butterfly, and let it inspire you.

HOPE IN THE LORD AND SOAR TO NEW HEIGHTS.

53

TREAT YOURSELF TO A CULTURAL EXPERIENCE.

Every artist dips into his own soul,
and paints his own nature
into his pictures.

A woman once took her young son to an art exhibit, unsure of exactly how he might respond to the imposing gallery, the crowd of adults, the silence of the great halls, and the pieces on display that defied comprehension. As they stood facing a modern painting, which may have been hung upside down for all the mother could tell, her son spoke up, "I like this one. It's how I feel sometimes."

Art, music, and dramatic performance speak to each person in different and sometimes unexpected ways, but they are always deep and wonderful. The artistic expressions of your culture convey the message that you are not alone in your feelings or isolated in your experiences.

THE ARTS SPEAK A UNIVERSAL LANGUAGE THAT CONNECTS US TO ONE ANOTHER.

54

BEGIN EACH DAY BY GIVING THANKS.

For all that has been, thanks!
For all that shall be, yes!

We are accustomed to giving thanks at the dinner table, but have you considered the benefits of doing so at the beginning of each day? Such an exercise can serve to guide you toward attitudes of love, forgiveness, and mercy. It will remind you that you are, even now, surrounded by blessings.

Begin today by thanking God for the simple things in life that bring you great joy. Thank Him for honest and useful work and the skill to perform it. Thank Him for the resources He has promised to meet your daily needs. Thank Him for the love of family and friends. And thank Him for the breath of life.

SAYING THANKS IS THE BEST WAY TO COUNT YOUR BLESSINGS.

55

BE CAREFUL NOT TO BITE OFF
MORE THAN YOU CAN CHEW.

*The wisdom of the prudent is to give
thought to their ways.*

PROVERBS 14:8

There is a point of diminishing return for all endeavors, where quantity conflicts with quality and pressure to perform conflicts with morale and good relationships. Overcommitment is a fast path to burnout. And no person can be truly happy if they are stressed to the max.

Many times overcommitment begins with good intentions. You want to help others and contribute to the world around you. However, it takes God's wisdom to determine which activities are right for you at any given time. None of us wants to be a Jack-of-all-trades and master of none.

In order to avoid feelings of hopelessness, it is vital to understand your limitations and abide by them.

CANDLES AREN'T MEANT TO BE BURNED AT BOTH ENDS.

56

TRUST IN THE GOODNESS
OF OTHERS.

Trust men and they will be true to you;
treat them greatly and
they will show themselves great.

The owners of a Florida restaurant instituted a "no bill" policy. At the end of the meal, diners were given "offering" envelopes. Over time, the owners discovered that some enclosed the true value of the meal, some left nothing or less than the meal's value, and some gave more than their meal cost to prepare and serve.

This might seem naive, and of course there were customers who took advantage of the opportunity to skip out and pay nothing. But overall, the trust that the owners placed in their customers was rewarded. And *everyone* felt good about it. There is a special joy in trusting people to do the right thing.

BELIEVING THE BEST
ABOUT PEOPLE DRAWS
THE BEST OUT OF THEM.

57

SAY "I LOVE YOU."

*Kind words can be short
and easy to speak,
but their echoes are truly endless.*

The paper was poorly folded. The writing was smudged and crooked. The verse didn't rhyme, and the cutout of a heart made less than a perfect Valentine. But the message from the young girl to her mother was clear: "I love you."

Don't wait to express your love for others. No matter how you package it, this gift is certain to bring renewed hope to your life and the lives of others. And failing to do so can bring you a heart full of dashed hopes when the opportunity is lost. It takes so little in the way of time, energy, and resources. Do it for yourself and someone you love today.

THE MOST IMPORTANT WORDS IN THE ENGLISH LANGUAGE ARE "I LOVE YOU."

58

GET PLENTY OF SLEEP.

Tired nature's sweet restorer,

balmy sleep!

During sleep the brain stays busy sorting and storing information, replenishing chemicals, and resolving problems or inequities. Scientists are not exactly sure how all this happens, but they are amazed by the amount and variety of activity that occurs while the body is at rest.

To get the most out of sleep hours, scientists recommend that you keep regular sleeping hours, get sufficient and regular exercise, quit smoking, limit caffeine, and refrain from overeating before going to bed. Sufficient rest will keep you at your best and make all your efforts more productive and more enjoyable.

EVERYTHING LOOKS BETTER WHEN YOU'VE HAD ENOUGH SLEEP.

59

REFUSE TO COMPARE
YOURSELF TO OTHERS.

Each of us is an original.

GALATIANS 5:26 THE MESSAGE

It's been said, "When God made you, He broke the mold." And though the expression is usually meant to be humorous, it's true! Since the beginning of time, and until the end of time, there will be only one you. This means that comparing yourself to others makes very little sense.

If you want to make a worthwhile comparison, try comparing yourself to yourself. Are you growing in positive ways? Using your talents to the best of your ability? Becoming someone you could look up to? Use your impulse to make comparisons as a self-improvement exercise. Why hopelessly strive to imitate someone you were never created to be?

WHY BE A COPY WHEN YOU ARE ALREADY AN ORIGINAL?

60

LEARN TO RECEIVE FROM OTHERS.

---

ow grateful I am and how
I praise the Lord
that you are helping me again.

PHILIPPIANS 4:10 TLB

When you acknowledge a gift as an expression of love, you give a gift of "appreciation" and loving "recognition" in return. An enthusiastic and thankful receiver creates an atmosphere of celebration for everyone and allows the giver to experience a moment of true joy.

Delight in every gift—whether small or large! Relish the party given in your honor—others will feel freer to enjoy themselves. Express appreciation when others come alongside to help—they will be more eager to help again. When you give someone else the opportunity to shine, your hope comes alive for them and you.

THOSE WHO RECEIVE WELL, GIVE A GIFT IN RETURN.

61

TRY A NEW FLAVOR OF ICE CREAM.

Pleasure in moderation relaxes and tempers the spirit.

Life's simple pleasures are often life's greatest pleasures. A new flavor of ice cream, a walk in the rain, a single fresh flower, a warm slice of homemade bread, taking time to watch an entire sunset unfold—each can be a delight to the senses and bring about a greater sense of well-being and hope.

Simple pleasures are those that don't need to be "saved for" or put off until vacation time. They are readily available to evoke the feelings of contentment and satisfaction that soothe frayed nerves. They give an extraordinary quality to otherwise ordinary days. And best of all, they nearly always can be shared.

I SCREAM, YOU SCREAM,
WE ALL SCREAM
FOR ICE CREAM!

62

LET OTHERS KNOW
WHEN YOU THINK GOOD
THOUGHTS ABOUT THEM.

Words are the soul's ambassadors,
who go abroad upon
her errands to and fro.

There is no better day than today for you to express the good thoughts you have for others. Too often we wait for special occasions to tell others what they mean to us, or that we are grateful for their presence in our lives. Whether it is simply to wish someone well, convey a sense of pride, or thank them for their kindness and support, your words only work if they are spoken.

When was the last time you told your spouse, your children, or one of your friends how much they mean to you? When you give someone else hope, your own level of hope rises.

IF YOU CAN'T SAY SOMETHING NICE, DON'T SAY ANYTHING; BUT IF YOU CAN SAY SOMETHING NICE, DO IT!

63

CHERISH EVERY
SPECIAL OCCASION.

It is right to celebrate.

LUKE 15:32 TLB

Rituals are important because they serve as markers for your life and relationships. Many people think that rituals are always religious in nature, but birthday parties, anniversary celebrations, award ceremonies, family gatherings, vacations, holiday dinners, even the fishing trips we take with a son or daughter are cultural rituals that unite us and enhance our connection with others.

Embrace the cultural rituals in your life. Take pictures and remember together. Memorialize family stories: "Hey do you remember when Grandpa . . . ?"

In the midst of daily hurdles, let your cherished memories encourage you. The same God who blessed you in the past is at work even now, planning more special occasions for you.

CELEBRATING SPECIAL OCCASIONS WITH THOSE WE LOVE BINDS OUR HEARTS TOGETHER.

64

PUT ASIDE PREJUDICE
AND STEREOTYPES.

---

*You must look into people as
well as at them.*

Prejudice and stereotypes are both blinding and binding. They keep you from experiences that can help you grow and develop character. Prejudice is not limited to ethnicity—it can be directed toward gender, age, economic status, and religion, to name just a few. One woman even admitted she was "prejudiced against those who are prejudiced."

On the flip side, putting aside prejudice can open wide the doors of friendship, peace, and cultural appreciation. It can expand the boundaries of our minds and enhance our knowledge of the world around us. Breaking the bonds of prejudice is like bursting forth from a cocoon to fly free and happy in the sunshine.

PREJUDICE CANNOT COEXIST
WITH LOVE. ONE WILL
ALWAYS PREVAIL TO THE
EXCLUSION OF THE OTHER.

65

SING IN THE SHOWER.

He who sings scares away his woes.

Luciano Pavarotti, Leontyne Price, Barbra Streisand, and others have become famous primarily because of their superb singing voices. They make it easy for you to close your eyes and be magically swept up in the emotions of happiness, love, and contentment.

Few are blessed with such talent, but most likely you can belt out a tune in the shower with the best of them. For a few happy moments, you can become one of the world's great singers, flooding the air with your own interpretations of personal favorites. Singing strengthens the lungs, exercises the diaphragm, and brings light to the soul. Try it, and see for yourself. A happy tune opens your heart to hope and bright expectations.

MAKING A JOYFUL NOISE CAN MAKE A JOYFUL HEART.

66

LISTEN TO THOSE WHO ARE WISE.

Apply your heart to instruction and your ears to words of knowledge.

PROVERBS 23:12

Depth perception tells us how close or far away certain objects are. Those with impaired vision in one eye lack accurate depth perception and have a decreased ability to make contact with or avoid objects.

The principle that two eyes are better than one extends far beyond physical eyesight. Wise mentors give us depth perception in regard to situations and circumstances. They help us make contact with success and stay out of harm's way. And when you consider that success is, to a certain extent, dependent upon the choices we make, it seems right to seek the advice of wise and caring people. When you do, hope for a bright future is well founded.

THE WISE NEVER STOP SEEKING WISDOM.

67

TRY A NEW RECIPE.

The discovery of a new dish does more for human happiness than the discovery of a new star.

The amazing and mysterious aspects of food have been known and appreciated since the beginning of recorded history. Just think of your own personal history and the association of wonderful meals with positive experiences. For example, holiday meals with family or that special restaurant dinner on the night you met someone special. Or "comfort food" associated with your childhood. All these examples show that food can be associated with good memories, but that it can also be used to make good memories. Food is very much a blessing of God.

So when you need a little boost, consider opening a recipe book and trying something daring and delicious. Today's cookbooks are simple enough for even the uninitiated to follow with ease. Invite a friend or loved one to your culinary adventure and make life hopeful again. *Bon appétit!*

DELIGHTING YOUR TASTE BUDS CAN SPICE UP YOUR DAY.

68

GIVE UP THE IDEA OF
CHANGING OTHERS.

*Consider how hard it is to change yourself
and you'll understand what
little chance you have of
trying to change others.*

One of the greatest and most liberating moments in life is the one when you realize you cannot change other people. No matter how much you love them or they love you—such change is entirely a function of personal will and God's grace.

Give love freely and unconditionally, accentuating the strengths and encouraging the good in those around you. Don't become an enabler of damaging behavior, but also remember that each person is ultimately responsible for their choices. People do change—often profoundly and genuinely—but such change must come from within, and often as a result of God's help. So set people and yourself free, and love them for who they are now. Then ask God for help. You'll feel a load lift and a renewed hope in what God can do to bring transformation.

THE ONLY ONE YOU CAN EFFECTIVELY CHANGE IS YOURSELF.

BE KIND TO A STRANGER.

I was a stranger, and ye took me in.

MATTHEW 25:35 KJV

An old tombstone reads, "He never met a stranger." What volumes that brief message conveys about the man buried there! It is easy to imagine that he was quick to laugh and quick to empathize, to the point of shedding a tear. It is easy to imagine his small acts of kindness to those who never knew the source of their "pleasant surprise."

What a great epitaph! What an avenue for inner fulfillment. Helping strangers is pure and unconditional. By its very nature, it has no strings attached. When you help a stranger, it serves as a gift of appreciation to God.

THERE ARE NO STRANGERS, ONLY PEOPLE WHO DON'T KNOW EACH OTHER YET.

70

LEARN SOME GOOD JOKES.

Laughter is the most beautiful
and beneficial therapy
God ever granted humanity.

Humor and its side effect, laughter, have been shown to improve both blood pressure and heart rate in seriously ill people. It is so therapeutic that clowns are permanent employees in most major children's hospitals. A little humor can heal broken relationships, defuse angry situations, and provide a much-needed change in perspective.

Invest some humor in your life by searching out and learning good jokes. They should be easy to remember and pass your own humor test. Never choose a joke that denigrates others—that is simply *not* funny. Stick with good taste and leave 'em rollin'.

BRIGHTEN YOUR DAY:
MAKE SOMEONE LAUGH.

71

RESPECT THE FEELINGS
OF OTHERS.

*The first duty of love
is to listen.*

Every person has a built-in need to be heard, understood, and respected. The key is to remember that respect is a sword that cuts two ways. What we need most comes to us as we give it away to others.

Learning to really listen and developing sensitivity to the needs of others is most often a matter of simple practice. When listening to others, learn to focus on them, and give them your full attention. Resist the urge to interrupt or mentally construct your reply, and don't give in to the temptation to judge or be their instructor when they just need a friend. Listening validates the speaker and conveys respect and caring. In giving, you shall receive.

RESPECT, WHETHER GIVEN OR RECEIVED, IS ITS OWN REWARD.

72

ALWAYS KEEP CONFIDENCES.

A gossip goes about telling secrets, but
one who is trustworthy
in spirit keeps a confidence.

PROVERBS 11:13 NRSV

Secrets can be wonderful and therapeutic. They can bring us great joy and emotional release. They can strengthen the bond between people and allow you to share in the happiness of others. Sharing of confidences can also mean that people trust you enough to make themselves vulnerable. When that happens, there is great virtue in keeping the confidence.

Protecting the secrets others confide in you is an expression of love. It is a guarding of relationship and a privileged responsibility. Its reward is a good night's sleep, strengthened character, and constant friendship. So keep your friends' secrets safe. Pray for the friends who have shared secret burdens, and you will find that your hope for them will give you a hope for your own life as well.

KEEPING SAFE THAT WHICH HAS BEEN COMMITTED UNTO YOU IS AN HONOR.

73

DEVELOP YOUR TALENTS.

A winner is someone who recognizes his talents, works his tail off to develop them, and uses them to achieve his goals.

Educational researchers have concluded that most people have between three and five major talents, each of which can be developed and applied in a way that will benefit others. Remember though, having talent is easy; developing that talent requires time, effort, and long-term commitment.

Discovering and developing your own specific talents can be one of the most fun and satisfying journeys of your life. The more you do what you were created to do, the greater your sense of fulfillment, purpose, and inner satisfaction. Your ability to hope grows with each accomplishment. Go ahead and mine your own gold!

PRACTICE ALWAYS BRINGS US CLOSER TO OUR OWN PERFECTION.

74

REFLECT ON GOD'S AWESOME UNIVERSE.

When I consider your heavens, the work of your fingers, the moon and the stars, which you have set in place, what is man that you are mindful of him, the son of man that you care for him?

PSALM 8:3-4

Childlike wonder is always in vogue. And wonder, we must, when we consider the vastness and splendor of the universe. The more we study its intricacies and delve into its mysteries, the more we are compelled to acknowledge that the "secret of life" and the "meaning of existence" cannot be reduced to an equation or formula. They are cradled lovingly in the hands of God.

So if it is hope that you truly desire, wander outside on a clear starlit night, and take a few moments or hours to gaze up into the cosmos. Allow your troubles to melt away as they are juxtaposed against a blanket of twinkling miracles.

LOOK UP AND SEE WHAT
GOD HAS DONE.

75

ALWAYS TELL THE TRUTH, THE WHOLE TRUTH, AND NOTHING BUT THE TRUTH.

Half the truth is often a great lie.

Contented people know better than to compromise the integrity of their souls for the sake of the moment. They cling to truthfulness and carefully guard their hearts from deception. Why? Because they have learned that telling the truth makes it easier to sleep at night, inspires the loyalty of friends, and earns the respect of all.

Nonetheless, honesty—pure and undiluted—is rare in our society today. It has fallen prey to convenience and a misguided belief that lying to people will help them in the end. Sure, truth is often painful, but the Bible says it can also be your best friend. Truth keeps you in God's light and brings you into closer fellowship with Him. That light and God's companionship along the way can bring you the hope that a life of integrity brings.

HONESTY REALLY IS
THE BEST POLICY.

76

BREAK DOWN YOUR DAY
INTO BITE-SIZED PIECES.

How do you eat an elephant?
One bite at a time.

One look at today's schedule and you're ready to climb back into bed. It seems overwhelmingly hopeless. But the day will seem more manageable if you take it one moment at a time. Think about a jigsaw puzzle. When you dump a thousand pieces onto the table, it looks like a mess, an overwhelming impossibility. But you start by finding the edge pieces, looking for corners, sorting by color, and slowly the final picture begins to take shape.

Today, break down big projects into smaller tasks. Handle only an hour at a time, if you have to. You will make it to your final destination, one step at a time.

EVERY STEP YOU TAKE
MAKES YOU CLOSER
TO YOUR GOAL.

77

STOP PLAYING THE LONE RANGER.

---

*Sticks in a bundle
are unbreakable.*

The Lone Ranger didn't defeat the bad guys alone. He had the help of his faithful friend Tonto, not to mention his lightning-fast horse Silver. People aren't designed to conquer life on their own. Whether it's moving furniture or battling depression, some situations require a call for help.

It's not always easy to ask for help, but remember, the help you need is available—whether it's physical, emotional, financial, or spiritual. It may take a little research and vulnerability to connect with the right counselor, friend, or family member, but sending up an SOS when you need it is a sure sign of maturity—not weakness. And your ultimate Helper—God—is always willing and ready to assist.

CONTINUALLY FLYING SOLO
CAN TAKE YOU SO LOW.

78

GO WITH GOD'S DESIGN.

How do you know what is going to happen tomorrow?

JAMES 4:14 TLB

Remember the last time you were disappointed? Things didn't turn out quite the way you expected, did they?

Sometimes this happens because we create an imaginary world in which forgetful friends never forget, picnics never get rained out, and loved ones always know the right gift to give us. Then when our expectations are upended, we feel shocked and appalled. But look a little closer at your disappointments. Is it reasonable to expect what you had set your heart upon? Why not go with reality here? Be willing to accommodate the way your loved ones are designed by temperament. Expect the possibility of rain on picnic days, and plan for it, just in case. And make the best of the way events play out. You will feel more hopeful going with God's flow in your life than if you attempt to create a rival reality to His.

YOU CAN'T CONTROL THE FUTURE, SO AVOID UNREALISTIC EXPECTATIONS.

79

LOVE THE UNLOVABLE.

It is not the most lovable individuals who stand more in need of love, but the most unlovable.

Jesus tells us to love our friends, our enemies, and everyone in between. Those "in-betweeners" include the annoying coworker who doesn't pull his weight, the ragged customer who reeks of alcohol, the woman with the disfigured face that everyone else turns away from. Is it *easy* to love people like that, to look them in the eye, to smile at them with genuine kindness, maybe even to hug them if that's what God wants us to do? No—not if we're relying solely on our own limited capabilities.

Loving the unlovable requires a supernatural helping of God's love. Imagine the hope you can bring to those who have only experienced rejection! You can't help but be encouraged yourself.

TO GOD, NO ONE
IS UNLOVABLE.

80

BECOME LIKE A LITTLE CHILD.

"Truly I tell you, unless you change
and become like children,
you will never enter the kingdom of heaven.
Whoever becomes humble like
this child is the greatest in the
kingdom of heaven."

MATTHEW 18:3-4 NRSV

We can learn a lot from children. Their carefree attitude and unending optimism are downright inspiring. Perhaps you remember a time when you viewed the world with wide-eyed wonder and felt the joy of complete abandon.

If you find yourself feeling hopeless today, take heart. Life's disappointments may have temporarily knocked you down, but you don't have to stay there. There is hope in God, and He will see you through.

Try this: go to a playground, find a swing, and abandon yourself to a time of pure, carefree play. As you fly through the air, picture all of your cares being swept away, yourself becoming freer with each pass. Delight in the Lord; He loves you!

NEVER OUTGROW
CHILD'S PLAY.

81

SHARE YOUR FAITH.

*"Go home to your friends, and
tell them how much
the Lord has done for you,
and what mercy he has shown you."*

MARK 5:19 NRSV

Some Christians are so afraid of the word *evangelism* that they clam up when the subject of faith arises in conversation. But if you think of Mark 5:19 as a prescription for evangelism, you'll find that sharing your faith is as simple as talking with a good friend.

Do you need to know a lot about theology? No. Do you need to have all the answers? Absolutely not—no one does anyway! Just tell the ones you love what you do know—what the Lord has done for you and how He has had mercy on you. You have a story about your experience with the Lord that no one else can tell. That's exciting! Just share your story.

THE GOOD NEWS IS
THE ULTIMATE HOPE!

82

VIEW LIFE AS AN ADVENTURE.

*The adventure of living has not
really begun until we stand
on our faith legs and claim . . .
the resources of our God.*

Webster's dictionary defines *adventure* as "an undertaking involving danger and unknown risks . . . an exciting or remarkable experience." What a great description of a Godly, hope-filled life! Yes, life is filled with hazards, and if you focus on them, you can miss the thrill of living the life God wants you to experience. You can end up playing it safe and leading a predictable—and often boring—existence. Even worse, you might never discover the life God intended for you to have.

Stand on your "faith legs," and grab hold of everything the Lord has for you. Decide never to squander another day. You don't have to journey to the far corners of the earth to find adventure. With God in your life, it's as close as your next step toward Him.

THE HOPE-FILLED LIFE IS
A LIFE OF ADVENTURE.

83

HUMBLE YOURSELF.

The spirit of God delights to dwell in the hearts of the humble.

How can humility keep hope alive? Humility is acknowledging that everything you have and everything you are is a result of God's work in your life. It is realizing that without Him you are nothing, but with Him *anything* is possible. As you humble yourself, yielding to Him more and more, your heart will become softer, more pliable, and teachable, causing you to grow. The more you acknowledge Him, the more it will bring Him glory and the more He can do in your life. It is a lifestyle that gets better and better.

WHEN YOU HUMBLE YOURSELF AND EXALT GOD, HE CAN WORK MIRACLES FOR YOU.

84

CONTROL YOUR TONGUE.

---

*So live that you wouldn't be
ashamed to sell the
family parrot to the town gossip.*

How does it feel to have your words parroted back to you? Often, not very good. Whenever we lose our temper, answer someone sarcastically, or repeat a choice morsel of gossip, we set ourselves up for trouble. What about the hurtful words we speak to those we love? Sticks and stones can break their bones, but words can crush the spirit.

And another misuse of the tongue is to say things like, "Oh, I can't do anything right" or "I'll never get out of debt." That only reinforces those notions and steers the course of your life on a self-defeating path. Get back on course by speaking positive words about yourself and others.

THE POWER OF LIFE AND DEATH IS IN YOUR TONGUE. USE IT WISELY.

85

BE A MENTOR.

"How can a student know more than his teacher? But if he works hard, he may learn as much."

LUKE 6:40 TLB

Well-known artist Thomas Kinkade tells of a neighbor who showed him in his youth what it took to be a successful artist. His neighbor was an art instructor who took the teenaged Thomas under his wing and allowed him to hang out in his studio. Many years and many millions of dollars later, Kinkade credits his former neighbor with giving him the encouragement and vision he needed to make his dream a reality.

Kinkade's neighbor was a true mentor. He spent time with one boy who showed promise. A mentor doesn't have to be a renowned artist, a professional, or an expert at anything. Children simply need the attention of a caring adult. Find some common ground, and invest in the life of a young person.

GIVE SOMEONE HOPE FOR A BRIGHTER FUTURE— GIVE YOURSELF.

86

FORGIVE AND FORGET.

*Forgiveness is not
an occasional act;
it is a permanent attitude.*

There's a wonderful story involving Clara Barton, who founded the American Red Cross. One time an acquaintance turned on her and humiliated her in front of a number of other people. Years later, a friend mentioned the incident to Clara, who seemed to have forgotten about it. Stunned, her friend questioned her, "Don't you remember it?" Clara responded, "No—I distinctly remember forgetting it."

Clara Barton had obviously not only forgiven her acquaintance but had also made a conscious decision to forget the offense. God has done likewise for us: when we confess our sins, He forgives us and then forgets about it. Shouldn't we do the same for those who offend us?

GOD WILL GIVE YOU THE GRACE TO FORGIVE AND THE ABILITY TO FORGET.

87

DEPEND COMPLETELY ON GOD.

---

*The more we depend on God,
the more dependable
we find He is.*

When you first begin a relationship with Jesus, you're like the fishermen of Galilee—you're asked to follow Him. However, as you come to know Him better, you realize that He is taking you to places where you must trust Him completely. Think of the miracle of the loaves and fishes. It was one thing to follow Jesus to the hillside, and it was quite another to be expected to feed thousands of hungry people with only a handful of food. Yet the disciples trusted Him, and no one went home hungry.

You can depend on Him in every circumstance that confronts you. Like the disciples, when you hope in him, you will not be left wanting.

DEVOTION TO CHRIST IS LIVED OUT IN DAILY DEPENDENCE ON HIM.

88

DANCE BEFORE THE LORD.

"I will build you up again and you will be rebuilt, O Virgin Israel. Again you will take up your tambourines and go out to dance with the joyful."

JEREMIAH 31:4

Many of us are not accustomed to thinking of dance as a form of worship. But historical records show that early Christians considered dancing before the Lord to be a normal part of worship. After all, they were a joyful people—why would they *not* dance?

It's difficult to dance before God if you only think of certain kinds of dance—ballroom or line dancing, for example. You can break out of that mold by putting on some praise songs and, with your arms outstretched toward God, simply move to the flow of the music. Turn, spin, sway, bow—it makes no difference. Close your eyes, and focus on the One who gave you the very ability to move. Honor God with your body's movement. Dance!

DAVID DANCED
BEFORE THE LORD—
AND SO CAN YOU.

89

THINK HOPE-FILLED THOUGHTS.

Why are you downcast, O my soul?

Why so disturbed within me?

Put your hope in God,

for I will yet praise him,

my Savior and my God.

PSALM 42:11

In the same way that we have to control our tongue, we also must control our thoughts. *What difference do thoughts make?* you may be wondering. What we choose to think about determines our perspective; our thoughts will be either a source of hope or a source of despair.

We can train our minds to think positively by capturing our negative thoughts and deliberately transforming them. *Oh, I am so alone—what a rare opportunity to spend time with God. The kids just won't settle down—they make my life so fulfilled that I would feel empty without them. The car needs a new battery—thanks, God, that I have a car to buy a battery for!* The level of hope you feel can be raised when you deliberately cultivate a positive outlook.

YOUR MIND IS LIKE A STOREHOUSE—FILL IT WITH GOOD THINGS.

90

RELAX.

Cast all your anxiety on him because he cares for you.

1 PETER 5:7

When you start to lose hope because you've allowed anxiety to creep in, it's an unmistakable signal to take time to relax.

First, find a comfortable place to recline, and then begin to replace your troubling thought with Bible verses about God's care and compassion. You'll be ready for some practical steps toward relaxing your body, since your mind and spirit are already in good hands. Focus on the parts of your body that are tense. In all likelihood, your face and shoulders are the primary culprits. Consciously tighten then relax each muscle in those areas. Keep going until your entire body is relaxed. And don't be in a hurry—stay like that for a while!

IT'S HARD TO BE HOPEFUL WHEN YOU'RE TIED UP IN KNOTS.

91

SEE WITH EYES OF FAITH.

All I have seen teaches me to
trust the Creator
for all I have not seen.

What does "seeing with eyes of faith," mean? It means visualizing what you are praying for long before you see the answer. It means seeing things from God's perspective.

Have you been praying for the salvation of a rebellious son? See him—through God's eyes—as a joyful young man committed to the things of God, a change God knows He can bring about through your prayers and His love. God sees your friend, a grief-stricken widow, on the day when He frees her from overwhelming sorrow. He knows the right place for your spouse, in a job that truly satisfies. Keep praying, believing, and seeing—with your eyes of faith. Your hope will grow as you see with God's eyes.

WHAT YOU CAN'T SEE IS OFTEN MORE REAL THAN WHAT YOU CAN SEE.

92

FALL IN LOVE—WITH GOD.

To fall in love with God is the greatest of all romances! To seek him is the greatest of all adventures! To find him is the greatest human achievement.

If you've ever been in love, you know how all consuming the passion is. The object of your love is the only person you want to be with, the only one you think about. Everything about that person thrills you.

Can you imagine feeling that way about the Lord? Maybe you were passionate about Him at one time, but the passion has cooled. Don't lose hope! You *can* fan the flame to get it burning brightly again. And if you've never experienced that kind of all-consuming fervor for the Lord, you can. Just admit your feelings to Him, and ask Him to give you a heart that is passionate for Him. It's a prayer He loves to answer.

WHEN YOU'RE IN LOVE WITH THE LORD, IT SEEMS THAT EVERYTHING IS RIGHT WITH THE WORLD.

93

FIX YOUR EYES ON JESUS.

L et us fix our eyes on Jesus,
the author and
perfecter of our faith.

HEBREWS 12:2

It is possible to become so inwardly focused that all you see are your shortcomings and failures. That will send you on a downward spiral, quenching all hope. But when you fix your eyes on Jesus, you are lifted up, and hope is restored.

Sure there are times you need to examine your heart, but that introspection should be short-lived and end on a positive note. God will never confront you in an abusive or condemning manner. If there are areas that need attention, the Holy Spirit will point them out, but He will always give you hope for change. He will even give you the strength to make those changes.

KEEP YOUR EYES ON JESUS.
IT WILL KEEP YOU LOOKING UP.

94

KEEP IT WHOLESOME.

Whatever is true, whatever is honorable, whatever is just, whatever is pure, whatever is pleasing, whatever is commendable, if there is any excellence and if there is anything worthy of praise, think about these things.

PHILIPPIANS 4:8 NRSV

Charles Swindoll writes of people today living in a moral fog. He notes that people are so accustomed to seeing and hearing moral standards violated that they seldom blush about it anymore. But that's no excuse for living anything less than a wholesome lifestyle. Swindoll believes that adhering to a high moral standard is such a serious matter to God that he imagines the Lord looking us in the eye and saying, "I want you to hear this very clearly. I'll make it brief and simple."

Don't allow sin to gain ground in your life. Make sure that whatever you watch, do, and say is pleasing to God.

IT'S HARD TO KEEP YOUR HOPES UP IF YOUR MIND IS IN THE GUTTER.

95

KEEP A BALANCED PERSPECTIVE.

The really idle man gets nowhere.
The perpetually busy man
does not get much farther.

With so many demands on our time, it's difficult to maintain a balanced lifestyle. But when life gets out of kilter, the resulting imbalance can erode your hope for the future. We need to establish priorities, but even that can be complicated.

Maybe you need to lose weight, so you decide to exercise three times a week before work. But that's when you pray and read the Bible. You could get up earlier, but then you'd lose the sleep you need. Go to bed earlier? You wish you could! Family demands make that nearly impossible.

Since God keeps the entire universe in order, and it never gets out of balance, surely He can give you creative ways to balance your priorities.

IT'S TRUE:
HE'S GOT THE WHOLE
WORLD IN HIS HANDS.

96

THRIVE ON SURPRISES.

My life is ending, I know that well,
but every day that is left me I feel
how my earthly life is in touch with a new infinite,
unknown, but approaching life, the nearness of
which sets my soul quivering with rapture, my mind
glowing, and my heart
weeping with joy.

Few things can lift a person's spirits like a good surprise. A preteen comes home from school on an ordinary Friday to discover that the family is going skiing for the weekend—and her best friend can come along. Or dessert is served *before* dinner to a wide-eyed, disbelieving youngster. Daily life is filled with opportunities to catch people off guard in ways that show how much you care about them.

God likes surprises too—He likes to surprise *you!* He might prompt an old friend to call you. You might balance the checkbook on the *first* try. Whatever it is, don't write off small blessings as coincidences. Everything is on purpose with God, even His abiding presence in your everyday events.

BE ALERT TO SURPRISES.
THEY ARE ALL AROUND YOU!

97

TRUST GOD WITH YOUR DEEPEST LONGINGS.

*All my longings lie open before you,
O Lord; my sighing
is not hidden from you.*

PSALM 38:9

Most people carry a dream. Perhaps you have carried one for so long that you have lost all hope of it ever coming to pass. But as a Christian you have the best hope to see your dreams become reality. The One who called the world into being is the same One who loves you and promises you abundant life.

Maybe you've hesitated to tell anyone, including God, what you long for. Maybe you're too sad or embarrassed or afraid. But the Bible says if you delight in the Lord, He will give you the desires of your heart (Psalm 37:4). Trusting Him with your dreams is one way to delight in Him. He won't let you down; and as you see what He can do, your hope will revive.

GOD IS WAITING FOR YOU TO TELL HIM YOUR DREAMS.

98

BREAK BAD HABITS.

*Now we can obey God's laws
if we follow after the
Holy Spirit and no longer obey
the old evil nature within us.*

ROMANS 8:4 TLB

Habits are hard to break. A good way to avoid discouragement and hopelessness is to avoid the pitfalls that can trap you. Spending within your budget, resisting the lure of pornography, and keeping your appetite in check can prevent a ton of suffering down the road. What seems harmless at first can often end up controlling your life. Don't give in to temptation!

Is it too late? Are you already trapped by a negative pattern of behavior? Once you realize that there's something you need to change—ask God for help. If you are addicted, you'll need support from loved ones. You might need to enlist the help of a counselor.

There is hope. You can change!

TEMPTATION WILL TAKE YOU FURTHER THAN YOU WANTED TO GO AND KEEP YOU THERE LONGER THAN YOU'D PLANNED.

99

EMBRACE THE UNEXPECTED.

None of us knows what the next change is going to be, what unexpected opportunity is just around the corner, waiting a few months or a few years to change all the tenor of our lives.

Sometimes we're hit with the unexpected, a "bend in the road," as author David Jeremiah calls it, that turns your world upside down. It can rattle you and cause you to lose your equilibrium. It helps to remember that to God nothing in our lives is unexpected. If we remember that fact, then hopelessness, fear, and emotional havoc cannot threaten further disruption.

Consider the possibility that the "unexpected" may actually be a part of God's perfect timing. Keep your eyes on Him. Let Him comfort you and walk with you and prepare you for the future. He promises to work out everything for your good, and your "bend in the road" may lead to an exciting opportunity that you can't see right now. If you'll take that promise to heart, you will live a life that is characterized as hopeful and filled with joyful expectancy.

WHAT YOU NEVER DARED TO HOPE FOR MAY BE RIGHT AROUND THE NEXT CORNER.

100

BECOME A CHEERLEADER.

The applause of a single human being is of great consequence.

If you've ever played any kind of competitive sport, you know the difference a cheering crowd can make. Your energy level rises, your confidence increases, your skill and ability improve. There's no question that when others root for you, you improve at what you do.

In everyday life, you have the chance to be a cheerleader, to let others experience the thrill of knowing someone is behind them 100 percent. Whether it's a friend, a spouse, or a child—*someone* out there needs to know you're rooting for them. Shout it loud—not literally, of course—but loud enough to be heard. A whispered encouragement may be all that's needed to inspire their hope and urge them on to success.

GIVING HOPE TO OTHERS WILL RESULT IN YOUR BEING CHEERED TOO.

101

APPRECIATE WHAT YOU HAVE.

Be satisfied with what you have.

HEBREWS 13:5 TLB

Many people spend their lives searching for happiness. In the end, some are fortunate enough to realize that it isn't about having more, doing more, or being more. It is about how you view what is already yours.

Look around you today, and appreciate the riches God has placed in your life. Even if your circumstances are troubling and your prospects slim, you can always revel in the vibrant colors of the morning sunrise or the amazing tenacity of a dandelion fighting to find its place in the sun. When you begin to see and appreciate the richness around you, you will almost certainly find that you have a great deal more to feel hopeful about than you once imagined.

APPRECIATING WHAT YOU
HAVE IS ONE WAY TO
KEEP YOUR HOPES UP.

ACKNOWLEDGEMENTS

(8) Robert Harold Schuller, (10) Aristotle, (12) Izaak Walton, (18) Alexander Pope, (20, 56, 66, 98, 106, 156) Author Unknown, (26) Oswald Chambers, (28) Louis Parrish, (32, 134) Miguel De Cervantes, (34) Peter Marshall, (38) Isaac Watts, (44, 110) Henry Ward Beecher, (46) Phaedrus, (50) Edward Stanley, (52) James Beattie, (58) Abraham Lincoln, (60) Roberta Culley, (62) George Herbert, (68) John Sullivan Dwight, (74) Terrance, (76) Elbert Hubbard, (78) William Shakespeare, (80, 126) Seneca, (84) Elizabeth Goudge, (86) Theodore Roosevelt, (90) Virginia Satir, (92, 116, 186) Ralph Waldo Emerson, (94) Robert Burns, (96) Zig Ziglar, (100) Francis Bacon, (104) Johann Paul Friedrich Richter, (112) Dag Hammarskjöld, (118) Mother Teresa of Calcutta, (120) Edward Young, (128) James Howell, (132) Lord Chesterfield, (138) Anthelme Brillat-Savarin, (140) Jacob M. Braude, (144) Charles R. Swindoll, (146) Paul Tillich, (150) Larry Bird, (154) Benjamin Franklin, (158) Kenyan Proverb, (162) Ashley Montagu, (168) Catherine Marshall, (170) Erasmus, (172) Will Rogers, (176) Martin Luther King Jr., (178) Cliff Richard, (188) Raphael Simon, (194) Sir Heneage Ogilvie, (196) Fyodor Dostoyevski, (202) Kathleen Norris, (204) Samuel Johnson.

Additional copies of this book
are available from your local bookstore.

The following titles are also available
in this series:
101 Simple Secrets to Keep Your Faith Alive
101 Simple Secrets to Keep Your Love Alive

If you have enjoyed this book,
or if it has impacted your life,
we would like to hear from you.
Please contact us at:
Honor Books
An Imprint of Cook Communications Ministries
4050 Lee Vance View
Colorado Springs, CO 80918
www.cookministries.com